Doombuster Wisdom

Meditations to Help You Save the World for Fun and Profit

By Roger Carlson

Doombuster Wisdom

Meditations to Help You Save the World for Fun and Profit

By Roger Carlson

Printed by Amazon KDP
Created and published through the Publishing to Profit Training Quote Book
Generator

Copyright 2019 Roger Carlson

Printed in the United States of America
10 9 8 7 6 5 4 3 2

Introduction

Gloom, despair, and agony on me
Deep, dark depression, excessive misery
If it weren't for bad luck, I'd have no luck at all
Gloom, despair, and agony on me

From the TV Show "Hee-Haw" (1969 -1992)

Warnings of doom can be good agents of change to avoid dangers and to inspire action, BUT as with all powerful agents, warnings can become a drug that brings fear, worry, and paralysis. World environmental warnings and scares have become a toxic addiction. The world society has been attacked with a cancer of hyper worry about the endless litany about famines, hothouse climate, resource exhaustion, resource shortages, enviro catastrophes from world famine to peak oil to global warming to rising sea levels. These are awesome scarifiers of doom.

This document is dedicated to a positive outlook on the future, one where every threatened doom is a chance to grow, an opportunity to dedicate ourselves to something greater by dreaming and building all the GREAT futures that 7 billion minds will create. Let us be inspired by past dreamers, like Buckminster Fuller and his geodesic domes, Arthur C. Clarke and his communication satellites, Jules Verne and his Nautilus; and the Steves (Jobs and Wozniak) with their personal computer.

Let us be encouraged by past writers, inventors and entrepreneurs who have saved the world from doom so many times. At the same time, we must remember that the inventor is a crackpot until such time as he or she succeeds. If we are to save the world, we must consider both dreams of success and possibilities of failure. The entrepreneur may risk all, and may even lose all for what seems a crackpot dream. Yet, some of those desperate ventures saved humanity and made fortunes for the entrepreneurs.

God watch over those entrepreneurs and us all!

"Believe you can and you're half way there."
-Theodore Roosevelt, U.S. president

Beginning Your Day

What does this quote mean to me personally today?

____

____

____

How will I apply this quote today?

____

____

____

Who else needs to hear this quote today?

____

____

____

At the End of Your Day

How did I apply this quote today?

____

____

____

What will I do differently going forward?

____

____

____

"Our deepest fear is not that we are inadequate. It is that we are powerful beyond our measure. It is our light, not our darkness that most frightens us. We ask ourselves, 'Who am I to be brilliant, gorgeous, talented, fabulous?' Actually, who are you not to be? Your playing small does not serve the world. There is nothing enlightened about shrinking so that other people won't feel insecure around you." -Marianne Williamson, metaphysical writer and speaker

Beginning Your Day

What does this quote mean to me personally today?

____

____

____

How will I apply this quote today?

____

____

____

Who else needs to hear this quote today?

____

____

____

At the End of Your Day

How did I apply this quote today?

____

____

____

What will I do differently going forward?

____

____

____

"Every vision is a joke until the first man accomplishes it; once realized, it becomes commonplace." -Robert H. Goddard, rocket pioneer

Beginning Your Day

What does this quote mean to me personally today?

____

____

____

How will I apply this quote today?

____

____

____

Who else needs to hear this quote today?

____

____

____

At the End of Your Day

How did I apply this quote today?

____

____

____

What will I do differently going forward?

____

____

____

"Ninety-nine percent of the failures come from people who have the habit of making excuses." -George Washington Carver, agricultural chemist, inventor of peanut butter & many other uses for peanuts

Beginning Your Day

What does this quote mean to me personally today?

____

____

____

How will I apply this quote today?

____

____

____

Who else needs to hear this quote today?

____

____

____

At the End of Your Day

How did I apply this quote today?

____

____

____

What will I do differently going forward?

____

____

____

"A goal without a date is just a dream." -Milton H. Erickson, hypnotherapist & pioneer in neurolinguistics programming

Beginning Your Day

What does this quote mean to me personally today?

____

____

____

How will I apply this quote today?

____

____

____

Who else needs to hear this quote today?

____

____

____

At the End of Your Day

How did I apply this quote today?

____

____

____

What will I do differently going forward?

____

____

____

"I'm not that smart. I'm just that focused." -Albert Einstein, physicist who developed the Theory of Relativity

Beginning Your Day

What does this quote mean to me personally today?

____

____

____

How will I apply this quote today?

____

____

____

Who else needs to hear this quote today?

____

____

____

At the End of Your Day

How did I apply this quote today?

____

____

____

What will I do differently going forward?

____

____

____

"You can never cross the ocean until you have the courage to lose sight of the shore." -Christopher Columbus, first well known European discoverer of America

Beginning Your Day

What does this quote mean to me personally today?

____

____

____

How will I apply this quote today?

____

____

____

Who else needs to hear this quote today?

____

____

____

At the End of Your Day

How did I apply this quote today?

____

____

____

What will I do differently going forward?

____

____

____

"Entrepreneurship is like a computer game in which you have to master every level before achieving success. Startups repeatedly stumble & have to go back to the drawing board. The best way to skip some levels and to increase the odds of survival is to learn from others who have already played the game." -Vivek Wadhwa, Indian-American software entrepreneur and theorist

Beginning Your Day

What does this quote mean to me personally today?

____

____

____

How will I apply this quote today?

____

____

____

Who else needs to hear this quote today?

____

____

____

At the End of Your Day

How did I apply this quote today?

____

____

____

What will I do differently going forward?

____

____

____

"If you accept the expectations of others, especially negative ones, then you never will change the outcome." -Michael Jordan, legendary disciplined and skilled basketball player

Beginning Your Day

What does this quote mean to me personally today?

____

____

____

How will I apply this quote today?

____

____

____

Who else needs to hear this quote today?

____

____

____

At the End of Your Day

How did I apply this quote today?

____

____

____

What will I do differently going forward?

____

____

____

"If we did all the things we are capable of, we would literally astound ourselves." -Thomas A. Edison, developer of the electric utility, electric light bulb, and other game changers

Beginning Your Day

What does this quote mean to me personally today?

How will I apply this quote today?

Who else needs to hear this quote today?

At the End of Your Day

How did I apply this quote today?

What will I do differently going forward?

"All that was great in the past was ridiculed, condemned, combated, suppressed - only to emerge all the more powerfully, all the more triumphantly from the struggle." -Nikola Tesla, inventor of alternating current & attempted inventor of much more

Beginning Your Day

What does this quote mean to me personally today?

____

____

____

How will I apply this quote today?

____

____

____

Who else needs to hear this quote today?

____

____

____

At the End of Your Day

How did I apply this quote today?

____

____

____

What will I do differently going forward?

____

____

____

"Look up at the stars and not down at your feet. Try to make sense of what you see, and wonder about what makes the universe exist. Be curious." -Stephen Hawking, physicist who studied black holes & continued his studies despite tremendous health challenges

Beginning Your Day

What does this quote mean to me personally today?

____

____

____

How will I apply this quote today?

____

____

____

Who else needs to hear this quote today?

____

____

____

At the End of Your Day

How did I apply this quote today?

____

____

____

What will I do differently going forward?

____

____

____

"Trying to do business without advertising is like winking at a pretty girl through a pair of green goggles. You may know what you are doing, but no one else does. Indomitable perseverance in a business, properly understood, always ensures ultimate success." -Cyrus McCormick, inventor of the mechanical reaper

Beginning Your Day

What does this quote mean to me personally today?

____

____

____

How will I apply this quote today?

____

____

____

Who else needs to hear this quote today?

____

____

____

At the End of Your Day

How did I apply this quote today?

____

____

____

What will I do differently going forward?

____

____

____

"You miss 100% of the shots you don't take."
-Wayne Gretzky, famous hockey player

Beginning Your Day

What does this quote mean to me personally today?

____

____

____

How will I apply this quote today?

____

____

____

Who else needs to hear this quote today?

____

____

____

At the End of Your Day

How did I apply this quote today?

____

____

____

What will I do differently going forward?

____

____

____

"If you really want to do something, you will find a way. If you don't, you'll find an excuse." -Jim Rohn, motivational speaker

Beginning Your Day

What does this quote mean to me personally today?

____

____

____

How will I apply this quote today?

____

____

____

Who else needs to hear this quote today?

____

____

____

At the End of Your Day

How did I apply this quote today?

____

____

____

What will I do differently going forward?

____

____

____

"Whoever would overthrow the liberty of a nation must begin by subduing the freeness of speech." -Benjamin Franklin, publisher, scientist, & co-author of the Declaration of Independence

Beginning Your Day

What does this quote mean to me personally today?

How will I apply this quote today?

Who else needs to hear this quote today?

At the End of Your Day

How did I apply this quote today?

What will I do differently going forward?

"To succeed, jump as quickly at opportunities as you do at conclusions." -Benjamin Franklin, publisher, scientist, & co-author of the Declaration of Independence

Beginning Your Day

What does this quote mean to me personally today?

____

____

____

How will I apply this quote today?

____

____

____

Who else needs to hear this quote today?

____

____

____

At the End of Your Day

How did I apply this quote today?

____

____

____

What will I do differently going forward?

____

____

____

"Success is not final, failure is not fatal; it is courage to continue that counts." -Winston Churchill, British prime minister who rallied the nation against a powerful German warlord who had conquered all of Europe

Beginning Your Day

What does this quote mean to me personally today?

How will I apply this quote today?

Who else needs to hear this quote today?

At the End of Your Day

How did I apply this quote today?

What will I do differently going forward?

"If you were born poor it's not your mistake, but if you die poor, it is your mistake." -Bill Gates, leader of Microsoft that dominated the computer revolution of the 1970s through 1990s

Beginning Your Day

What does this quote mean to me personally today?

____

____

____

How will I apply this quote today?

____

____

____

Who else needs to hear this quote today?

____

____

____

At the End of Your Day

How did I apply this quote today?

____

____

____

What will I do differently going forward?

____

____

____

"A seed planted in the ground does not feel its lack of roots, stem and petals as a 'weakness' or being 'less than'. It simply sees an opportunity to grow and then does." -Michael Stevenson, neurolinguistic programming language trainer

Beginning Your Day

What does this quote mean to me personally today?

____

____

____

How will I apply this quote today?

____

____

____

Who else needs to hear this quote today?

____

____

____

At the End of Your Day

How did I apply this quote today?

____

____

____

What will I do differently going forward?

____

____

____

"It's not about money or connections, it's the willingness to outwork and outlearn everyone when it comes to your business. And if it fails, you learn from what happened and do a better job next time." -Mark Cuban, investor and owner of the Dallas Mavericks

Beginning Your Day

What does this quote mean to me personally today?

____

____

____

How will I apply this quote today?

____

____

____

Who else needs to hear this quote today?

____

____

____

At the End of Your Day

How did I apply this quote today?

____

____

____

What will I do differently going forward?

____

____

____

"The best way to predict the future is to create it." -Peter Drucker, management consultant

Beginning Your Day

What does this quote mean to me personally today?

____

____

____

How will I apply this quote today?

____

____

____

Who else needs to hear this quote today?

____

____

____

At the End of Your Day

How did I apply this quote today?

____

____

____

What will I do differently going forward?

____

____

____

"Adversity has the effect of eliciting talents, which, in prosperous circumstances would have lain dormant." -Horace, ancient Roman poet

Beginning Your Day

What does this quote mean to me personally today?

____

____

____

How will I apply this quote today?

____

____

____

Who else needs to hear this quote today?

____

____

____

At the End of Your Day

How did I apply this quote today?

____

____

____

What will I do differently going forward?

____

____

____

"Our shadow selves of fear and wild imaginings have the idea seeds that our more positive selves can harness for prosperity beyond measure. Ideas plus work make innovations. That is the way it has always been from the first people chipping stones into spear points to those building computers today. " -Roger Carlson

Beginning Your Day

What does this quote mean to me personally today?

How will I apply this quote today?

Who else needs to hear this quote today?

At the End of Your Day

How did I apply this quote today?

What will I do differently going forward?

"Any sufficiently advanced technology is indistinguishable from magic." -Arthur C. Clarke, science fiction author, futurist, and inventor of the geosynchronous communications satellite

Beginning Your Day

What does this quote mean to me personally today?

____

____

____

How will I apply this quote today?

____

____

____

Who else needs to hear this quote today?

____

____

____

At the End of Your Day

How did I apply this quote today?

____

____

____

What will I do differently going forward?

____

____

____

"I can't change the direction of the wind, but I can adjust my sails to always reach my destination." -Jimmy Dean, country western singer

Beginning Your Day

What does this quote mean to me personally today?

____

____

____

How will I apply this quote today?

____

____

____

Who else needs to hear this quote today?

____

____

____

At the End of Your Day

How did I apply this quote today?

____

____

____

What will I do differently going forward?

____

____

____

"Strong minds discuss ideas, average minds discuss events, weak minds discuss people." -Socrates, ancient Greek philosopher

Beginning Your Day

What does this quote mean to me personally today?

____

____

____

How will I apply this quote today?

____

____

____

Who else needs to hear this quote today?

____

____

____

At the End of Your Day

How did I apply this quote today?

____

____

____

What will I do differently going forward?

____

____

____

"New ideas pass through three periods: 1) It can't be done. 2) It probably can be done, but it's not worth doing. 3) I knew it was a good idea all along!" -Arthur C. Clarke, science fiction author, futurist, and inventor of the geosynchronous communications satellite

Beginning Your Day

What does this quote mean to me personally today?

How will I apply this quote today?

Who else needs to hear this quote today?

At the End of Your Day

How did I apply this quote today?

What will I do differently going forward?

"Tell me and I forget. Teach me and I remember. Involve me and I learn." -Benjamin Franklin, publisher, scientist, & co-author of the Declaration of Independence

Beginning Your Day

What does this quote mean to me personally today?

____

____

____

How will I apply this quote today?

____

____

____

Who else needs to hear this quote today?

____

____

____

At the End of Your Day

How did I apply this quote today?

____

____

____

What will I do differently going forward?

____

____

____

"Your journey has molded you for your greater good, and it was exactly what it needed to be. Don't think that you've lost time. It took each and every situation you have encountered to bring you to the now. And now is right on time." -Asha Tyson, motivational speaker

Beginning Your Day

What does this quote mean to me personally today?

____

____

____

How will I apply this quote today?

____

____

____

Who else needs to hear this quote today?

____

____

____

At the End of Your Day

How did I apply this quote today?

____

____

____

What will I do differently going forward?

____

____

____

"Pollution is nothing but the resources we are not harvesting. We allow them to disperse because we've been ignorant of their value." -R. Buckminster Fuller, designer and futurist, popularizer of the geodesic dome

Beginning Your Day

What does this quote mean to me personally today?

How will I apply this quote today?

Who else needs to hear this quote today?

At the End of Your Day

How did I apply this quote today?

What will I do differently going forward?

"You can't have a better tomorrow if you are always thinking about yesterday." -Charles F. Kettering, inventor of the electric starter for cars

Beginning Your Day

What does this quote mean to me personally today?

____

____

____

How will I apply this quote today?

____

____

____

Who else needs to hear this quote today?

____

____

____

At the End of Your Day

How did I apply this quote today?

____

____

____

What will I do differently going forward?

____

____

____

"Be grateful for what you have and stop complaining. It bores everyone else, does you no good, and doesn't solve any problems." -Zig Zigler, author, salesman, and motivational speaker

Beginning Your Day

What does this quote mean to me personally today?

____

____

____

How will I apply this quote today?

____

____

____

Who else needs to hear this quote today?

____

____

____

At the End of Your Day

How did I apply this quote today?

____

____

____

What will I do differently going forward?

____

____

____

"Live as if you were to die tomorrow. Learn as if you were to live forever." -Mahatma Gandhi, liberator of India

Beginning Your Day

What does this quote mean to me personally today?

____

____

____

How will I apply this quote today?

____

____

____

Who else needs to hear this quote today?

____

____

____

At the End of Your Day

How did I apply this quote today?

____

____

____

What will I do differently going forward?

____

____

____

"You can get everything in life you want if you will just help enough other people get what they want." -Zig Zigler, author, salesman, and motivational speaker

Beginning Your Day

What does this quote mean to me personally today?

How will I apply this quote today?

Who else needs to hear this quote today?

At the End of Your Day

How did I apply this quote today?

What will I do differently going forward?

"If it scares you, it might be a good thing to try." -Seth Godin, author and former dot com business executive

Beginning Your Day

What does this quote mean to me personally today?

____

____

____

How will I apply this quote today?

____

____

____

Who else needs to hear this quote today?

____

____

____

At the End of Your Day

How did I apply this quote today?

____

____

____

What will I do differently going forward?

____

____

____

"It's kind of fun to do the impossible." -Walt Disney, made the first animated feature film (Snow White), founded Disneyland

Beginning Your Day

What does this quote mean to me personally today?

____

____

____

How will I apply this quote today?

____

____

____

Who else needs to hear this quote today?

____

____

____

At the End of Your Day

How did I apply this quote today?

____

____

____

What will I do differently going forward?

____

____

____

"If we were logical, the future would be bleak, indeed. But we are more than logical. We are human beings, and we have faith, and we have hope, and we can work." -Jacques Yves Cousteau, oceanic explorer and popularizer

Beginning Your Day
What does this quote mean to me personally today?

How will I apply this quote today?

Who else needs to hear this quote today?

At the End of Your Day
How did I apply this quote today?

What will I do differently going forward?

"I predict future happiness for Americans, if they can prevent the government from wasting the labors of the people under the pretense of taking care of them." -Thomas Jefferson, primary author of the Declaration of independence, third president of the United States

Beginning Your Day

What does this quote mean to me personally today?

How will I apply this quote today?

Who else needs to hear this quote today?

At the End of Your Day

How did I apply this quote today?

What will I do differently going forward?

"There is little success where there is little laughter." -Andrew Carnegie, steel magnate, philanthropist

Beginning Your Day

What does this quote mean to me personally today?

How will I apply this quote today?

Who else needs to hear this quote today?

At the End of Your Day

How did I apply this quote today?

What will I do differently going forward?

"If you hear a voice within you say you cannot paint, then by all means, paint, and that voice will be silenced." -Vincent Van Gogh, artist

Beginning Your Day

What does this quote mean to me personally today?

How will I apply this quote today?

Who else needs to hear this quote today?

At the End of Your Day

How did I apply this quote today?

What will I do differently going forward?

"Do not let the hero in your soul perish, in lonely frustration, for the life you deserved but never have been able to reach. Check your road and the nature of your battle. The world you desired can be won. It exists, it is real, it is possible, it is yours." -John Galt, character in Atlas Shrugged by Ayn Rand

Beginning Your Day

What does this quote mean to me personally today?

____

____

____

How will I apply this quote today?

____

____

____

Who else needs to hear this quote today?

____

____

____

At the End of Your Day

How did I apply this quote today?

____

____

____

What will I do differently going forward?

____

____

____

"I'd rather regret the things I've done, than regret the things I haven't done." -Lucille Ball, comedian

Beginning Your Day

What does this quote mean to me personally today?

____

____

____

How will I apply this quote today?

____

____

____

Who else needs to hear this quote today?

____

____

____

At the End of Your Day

How did I apply this quote today?

____

____

____

What will I do differently going forward?

____

____

____

"Don't let the fear of striking out hold you back." -Babe Ruth, baseball player famous for hitting home runs

Beginning Your Day

What does this quote mean to me personally today?

____

____

____

How will I apply this quote today?

____

____

____

Who else needs to hear this quote today?

____

____

____

At the End of Your Day

How did I apply this quote today?

____

____

____

What will I do differently going forward?

____

____

____

"Listen to the mustnts, child. Listen to the don'ts. Listen to the shouldnts, the impossibles, the won'ts. Listen to the never haves, THEN listen close to me? Anything can happen, child. Anything can be." -Shel Silverstein, poet and songwriter

Beginning Your Day

What does this quote mean to me personally today?

How will I apply this quote today?

Who else needs to hear this quote today?

At the End of Your Day

How did I apply this quote today?

What will I do differently going forward?

"My playmates never failed to wink and smile mockingly at me when one of them called 'Man flies!' for at the word I would always lift my finger very high, as a sign of absolute conviction; and I refused with energy to pay the forfeit. The more they laughed at me, the happier I was, hoping that some day the laugh would be on my side." -Santos Dumont, aviation pioneer

Beginning Your Day
What does this quote mean to me personally today?

____

____

____

How will I apply this quote today?

____

____

____

Who else needs to hear this quote today?

____

____

____

At the End of Your Day
How did I apply this quote today?

____

____

____

What will I do differently going forward?

____

____

____

"Man will never fly! But if someone does, it will not be anyone from Dayton, Ohio!" -Old man standing outside of the Wright Brothers bicycle shop in Dayton, Ohio

Beginning Your Day

What does this quote mean to me personally today?

____

____

____

How will I apply this quote today?

____

____

____

Who else needs to hear this quote today?

____

____

____

At the End of Your Day

How did I apply this quote today?

____

____

____

What will I do differently going forward?

____

____

____

"The only way to permanently change the temperature in the room is to reset the thermostat. In the same way, the only way to change your level of financial success 'permanently' is to reset your financial thermostat. But it is your choice whether you choose to change." -T. Harv Eker, motivational speaker

Beginning Your Day

What does this quote mean to me personally today?

____

____

____

How will I apply this quote today?

____

____

____

Who else needs to hear this quote today?

____

____

____

At the End of Your Day

How did I apply this quote today?

____

____

____

What will I do differently going forward?

____

____

____

"We are at the very beginning of time for the human race. It is not unreasonable that we grapple with problems. But there are tens of thousands of years in the future. Our responsibility is to do what we can, learn what we can, improve the solutions, and pass them on."
-Richard P. Feynman, funny & good man, physicist, Nobel Prize winner

Beginning Your Day
What does this quote mean to me personally today?

____

____

____

How will I apply this quote today?

____

____

____

Who else needs to hear this quote today?

____

____

____

At the End of Your Day
How did I apply this quote today?

____

____

____

What will I do differently going forward?

____

____

____

"A successful man will profit from his mistakes and try again in a different way." -Dale Carnegie, speech and leadership trainer

Beginning Your Day

What does this quote mean to me personally today?

____

____

____

How will I apply this quote today?

____

____

____

Who else needs to hear this quote today?

____

____

____

At the End of Your Day

How did I apply this quote today?

____

____

____

What will I do differently going forward?

____

____

____

"The dangers of not thinking clearly are much greater now than ever before. It's not that there's something new in our way of thinking - it's that credulous and confused thinking can be much more lethal in ways it was never before." -Carl Sagan, astronomer and philosopher

Beginning Your Day

What does this quote mean to me personally today?

____

____

____

How will I apply this quote today?

____

____

____

Who else needs to hear this quote today?

____

____

____

At the End of Your Day

How did I apply this quote today?

____

____

____

What will I do differently going forward?

____

____

____

"Science fiction writers foresee the inevitable, and although problems and catastrophes may be inevitable, solutions are not." -Isaac Asimov, writer of both science and science fiction

Beginning Your Day

What does this quote mean to me personally today?

How will I apply this quote today?

Who else needs to hear this quote today?

At the End of Your Day

How did I apply this quote today?

What will I do differently going forward?

"Progress is impossible without change, and those who cannot change their minds cannot change anything." -George Bernard Shaw, playwright

Beginning Your Day

What does this quote mean to me personally today?

____

____

____

How will I apply this quote today?

____

____

____

Who else needs to hear this quote today?

____

____

____

At the End of Your Day

How did I apply this quote today?

____

____

____

What will I do differently going forward?

____

____

____

"Life is a series of experiences, each one of which makes us bigger, even though sometimes it is hard to realize this. For the world was built to develop character, and we must learn that the setbacks and grieves which we endure help us in our marching onward." -Henry Ford, founder of Ford Motor Company, developer of the Model T (the first car affordable by working families)

Beginning Your Day
What does this quote mean to me personally today?

How will I apply this quote today?

Who else needs to hear this quote today?

At the End of Your Day
How did I apply this quote today?

What will I do differently going forward?

"Vision is the art of seeing what is invisible to others." -Jonathan Swift, satirist

Beginning Your Day

What does this quote mean to me personally today?

____

How will I apply this quote today?

____

Who else needs to hear this quote today?

____

At the End of Your Day

How did I apply this quote today?

____

What will I do differently going forward?

____

"When people have their own money at stake, it's a lot easier to find and settle on practical, no-nonsense solutions to engineering problems than is ever the case in the complex and endless deliberations of a government bureaucracy." -Robert Zubrin, aerospace pioneer and proponent of Mars settlement

Beginning Your Day
What does this quote mean to me personally today?

____

____

____

How will I apply this quote today?

____

____

____

Who else needs to hear this quote today?

____

____

____

At the End of Your Day
How did I apply this quote today?

____

____

____

What will I do differently going forward?

____

____

____

"Sometimes if you want to see a change for the better, you have to take things into your own hands." -Clint Eastwood, actor and director

Beginning Your Day

What does this quote mean to me personally today?

____
____
____

How will I apply this quote today?

____
____
____

Who else needs to hear this quote today?

____
____
____

At the End of Your Day

How did I apply this quote today?

____
____
____

What will I do differently going forward?

____
____
____

"Nothing is impossible, the word itself says 'I'm possible!" -Audrey Hepburn, actress

Beginning Your Day

What does this quote mean to me personally today?

How will I apply this quote today?

Who else needs to hear this quote today?

At the End of Your Day

How did I apply this quote today?

What will I do differently going forward?

"Averting a looming (pick favorite) catastrophe, crisis, etc., requires us to hew to their worldview, in which we are the problem & the Earth is to be saved. Environmental groups routinely preach doom. They claim technology is dangerous & industrial development must be stopped to the save the planet. Yet, they are trying to stop innovations that improve the environment & raise the living standards." -Robert Bryce, energy analyst

Beginning Your Day

What does this quote mean to me personally today?

How will I apply this quote today?

Who else needs to hear this quote today?

At the End of Your Day

How did I apply this quote today?

What will I do differently going forward?

"If your actions inspire others to dream more, learn more, do more and become more, you are a leader." -John Quincy Adams, Sixth United States president

Beginning Your Day

What does this quote mean to me personally today?

____

____

____

How will I apply this quote today?

____

____

____

Who else needs to hear this quote today?

____

____

____

At the End of Your Day

How did I apply this quote today?

____

____

____

What will I do differently going forward?

____

____

____

"If you want to succeed you should strike out on new paths, rather than travel the worn paths of accepted success." -John D. Rockefeller, greatest oil magnate of all time

Beginning Your Day

What does this quote mean to me personally today?

____

____

How will I apply this quote today?

____

____

Who else needs to hear this quote today?

____

____

At the End of Your Day

How did I apply this quote today?

____

____

What will I do differently going forward?

____

____

"Being a monopoly, govt brings inefficiency & stagnation to most things it runs; govt agencies pursue inflation of their budgets rather than service to customers & pressure groups form unholy alliances with agencies to extract more from taxpayers. Despite all this, most people still call for govt to run more things & assume that it would somehow be more perfect, more selfless, next time." -Matt Ridley, author of The Rational Optimist: How Prosperity Evolves

Beginning Your Day

What does this quote mean to me personally today?

____

____

____

How will I apply this quote today?

____

____

____

Who else needs to hear this quote today?

____

____

____

At the End of Your Day

How did I apply this quote today?

____

____

____

What will I do differently going forward?

____

____

____

"Integrity is everything. With it, you can weather all storms. Without it, even little things will derail you. Hold true to your commitments because relationships are either built or undone by them." -Michael Stevenson, trainer in hypnotism, neurolinguistics programming language, and business

Beginning Your Day

What does this quote mean to me personally today?

____

____

____

How will I apply this quote today?

____

____

____

Who else needs to hear this quote today?

____

____

____

At the End of Your Day

How did I apply this quote today?

____

____

____

What will I do differently going forward?

____

____

____

"Mystery creates wonder and wonder is the basis of man's desire to understand." -Neil Armstrong, first man on the Moon

Beginning Your Day

What does this quote mean to me personally today?

____

____

____

How will I apply this quote today?

____

____

____

Who else needs to hear this quote today?

____

____

____

At the End of Your Day

How did I apply this quote today?

____

____

____

What will I do differently going forward?

____

____

____

"In wisdom gathered over time I have found that every experience is a form of exploration." -Ansel Adams, nature photographer

Beginning Your Day

What does this quote mean to me personally today?

How will I apply this quote today?

Who else needs to hear this quote today?

At the End of Your Day

How did I apply this quote today?

What will I do differently going forward?

"The size of your success is measured by the strength of your desire; the size of your dream; and how you handle disappointment along the way." -Robert Kiyosaki, educator on business and personal finance

Beginning Your Day

What does this quote mean to me personally today?

____

____

____

How will I apply this quote today?

____

____

____

Who else needs to hear this quote today?

____

____

____

At the End of Your Day

How did I apply this quote today?

____

____

____

What will I do differently going forward?

____

____

____

"A primary reason that people believe that life is getting worse is because our information about the problems of the world has steadily improved. If there is a battle today somewhere on the planet, we experience it almost as if we were there." -Ray Kurzweil, futurist, author of The Singularity Is Near: When Humans Transcend Biology

Beginning Your Day

What does this quote mean to me personally today?

____

____

____

How will I apply this quote today?

____

____

____

Who else needs to hear this quote today?

____

____

____

At the End of Your Day

How did I apply this quote today?

____

____

____

What will I do differently going forward?

____

____

____

"You're going to go through tough times ? that's life. But I say, 'Nothing happens to you, it happens for you.' See the positive in negative events." -Joel Osteen, preacher

Beginning Your Day

What does this quote mean to me personally today?

____

____

____

How will I apply this quote today?

____

____

____

Who else needs to hear this quote today?

____

____

____

At the End of Your Day

How did I apply this quote today?

____

____

____

What will I do differently going forward?

____

____

____

"Right now, and for the first time ever, a passionate and committed individual has access to the technology, minds, and capital required to take on any challenge." -Peter H. Diamandis, author of Bold: How to Go Big, Create Wealth and Impact the World

Beginning Your Day

What does this quote mean to me personally today?

____

____

____

How will I apply this quote today?

____

____

____

Who else needs to hear this quote today?

____

____

____

At the End of Your Day

How did I apply this quote today?

____

____

____

What will I do differently going forward?

____

____

____

"Sometimes, I wonder if the world is being run by smart people who are putting us on or by fools who really mean it." -Mark Twain, novelist and humorist

Beginning Your Day

What does this quote mean to me personally today?

____

____

____

How will I apply this quote today?

____

____

____

Who else needs to hear this quote today?

____

____

At the End of Your Day

How did I apply this quote today?

____

____

____

What will I do differently going forward?

____

____

____

"I do not believe in circumstances. The people who get on in this world are the people who get up and look for the circumstances they want, and, if they can't find them, make them." -George Bernard Shaw, playwright

Beginning Your Day

What does this quote mean to me personally today?

____

____

____

How will I apply this quote today?

____

____

____

Who else needs to hear this quote today?

____

____

____

At the End of Your Day

How did I apply this quote today?

____

____

____

What will I do differently going forward?

____

____

____

"It is better to lead from behind and to put others in front, especially when you celebrate victory when nice things occur. You take the front line when there is danger. Then people will appreciate your leadership." -Nelson Mandela, liberator of South Africa from apartheid

Beginning Your Day

What does this quote mean to me personally today?

____

____

____

How will I apply this quote today?

____

____

____

Who else needs to hear this quote today?

____

____

____

At the End of Your Day

How did I apply this quote today?

____

____

____

What will I do differently going forward?

____

____

____

"Do not believe everything you read on the Internet just because it has a picture next to it." -Abraham Lincoln [Whoever said it, the morale is to be skeptical and check.]

Beginning Your Day

What does this quote mean to me personally today?

____

____

____

How will I apply this quote today?

____

____

____

Who else needs to hear this quote today?

____

____

____

At the End of Your Day

How did I apply this quote today?

____

____

____

What will I do differently going forward?

____

____

____

"If you really look closely, most overnight successes took a long time." -Steve Jobs, co-founder of Apple Computer, developer of the I-phone

Beginning Your Day

What does this quote mean to me personally today?

How will I apply this quote today?

Who else needs to hear this quote today?

At the End of Your Day

How did I apply this quote today?

What will I do differently going forward?

"Fall seven times and stand up eight." -Japanese proverb

Beginning Your Day

What does this quote mean to me personally today?

____

____

____

How will I apply this quote today?

____

____

____

Who else needs to hear this quote today?

____

____

____

At the End of Your Day

How did I apply this quote today?

____

____

____

What will I do differently going forward?

____

____

____

"A successful man is one who can lay a firm foundation with the bricks that others throw at him." -David Brinkley, television newscaster

Beginning Your Day

What does this quote mean to me personally today?

____

____

____

How will I apply this quote today?

____

____

____

Who else needs to hear this quote today?

____

____

____

At the End of Your Day

How did I apply this quote today?

____

____

____

What will I do differently going forward?

____

____

____

"To effectively communicate, we must realize that we are all different in the way we perceive the world and use this understanding as a guide to our communication with others." -Tony Robbins, inspirational speaker and author

Beginning Your Day

What does this quote mean to me personally today?

____

____

____

How will I apply this quote today?

____

____

____

Who else needs to hear this quote today?

____

____

____

At the End of Your Day

How did I apply this quote today?

____

____

____

What will I do differently going forward?

____

____

____

"Don't find fault, find a remedy." -Henry Ford, founder of Ford Motor Company, developer of the Model T (the first car affordable by common families)

Beginning Your Day

What does this quote mean to me personally today?

How will I apply this quote today?

Who else needs to hear this quote today?

At the End of Your Day

How did I apply this quote today?

What will I do differently going forward?

"We may be at a point of peak oil production." -Former President Bill Clinton at the London Business School March 28, 2006 [Clinton was merely repeating the view of many oil experts at the time]

Beginning Your Day

What does this quote mean to me personally today?

____

____

____

How will I apply this quote today?

____

____

____

Who else needs to hear this quote today?

____

____

____

At the End of Your Day

How did I apply this quote today?

____

____

____

What will I do differently going forward?

____

____

____

"Do the one thing you think you cannot do. Fail at it. Try again. Do better the second time. The only people who never tumble are those who never mount the high wire. This is your moment. Own it." -Oprah Winfrey, television interviewer

Beginning Your Day
What does this quote mean to me personally today?

How will I apply this quote today?

Who else needs to hear this quote today?

At the End of Your Day
How did I apply this quote today?

What will I do differently going forward?

"Open your eyes, look within. Are you satisfied with the life you're living?" -Bob Marley, superstar reggae musician

Beginning Your Day

What does this quote mean to me personally today?

____

____

____

How will I apply this quote today?

____

____

____

Who else needs to hear this quote today?

____

____

____

At the End of Your Day

How did I apply this quote today?

____

____

____

What will I do differently going forward?

____

____

____

"If I were a gambler, I would take even money that England will not exist in the year 2000." -Paul R. Ehrlich, entomologist & self-proclaimed population expert, 1969 [P.S.: England still exists]

Beginning Your Day

What does this quote mean to me personally today?

How will I apply this quote today?

Who else needs to hear this quote today?

At the End of Your Day

How did I apply this quote today?

What will I do differently going forward?

"Our greatest weakness lies in giving up. The most certain way to succeed is always to try just one more time." -Thomas A. Edison, developer of the electric utility, electric light bulb, and other game changers

Beginning Your Day

What does this quote mean to me personally today?

____

____

____

How will I apply this quote today?

____

____

____

Who else needs to hear this quote today?

____

____

____

At the End of Your Day

How did I apply this quote today?

____

____

____

What will I do differently going forward?

____

____

____

"Give me a lever long enough and a fulcrum on which to place it, and I shall move the world." -Archimedes, ancient Greek mathematician

Beginning Your Day

What does this quote mean to me personally today?

____

____

____

How will I apply this quote today?

____

____

____

Who else needs to hear this quote today?

____

____

____

At the End of Your Day

How did I apply this quote today?

____

____

____

What will I do differently going forward?

____

____

____

"I have learned over the years that when one's mind is made up, that diminishes fear; knowing what must be done does away with fear." -Rosa Parks, civil rights activist

Beginning Your Day

What does this quote mean to me personally today?

How will I apply this quote today?

Who else needs to hear this quote today?

At the End of Your Day

How did I apply this quote today?

What will I do differently going forward?

"The trick to getting ahead is getting started." -Mark Twain, novelist and humorist

Beginning Your Day

What does this quote mean to me personally today?

How will I apply this quote today?

Who else needs to hear this quote today?

At the End of Your Day

How did I apply this quote today?

What will I do differently going forward?

"If you can dream it, you can do it." -Walt Disney, made the first animated feature film (Snow White), founded Disneyland

Beginning Your Day

What does this quote mean to me personally today?

____
____
____

How will I apply this quote today?

____
____
____

Who else needs to hear this quote today?

____
____
____

At the End of Your Day

How did I apply this quote today?

____
____
____

What will I do differently going forward?

____
____
____

"The starting point of all achievement is desire." -Napoleon Hill, inspirational writer and speaker, author of Think and Grow Rich

Beginning Your Day

What does this quote mean to me personally today?

____

____

____

How will I apply this quote today?

____

____

____

Who else needs to hear this quote today?

____

____

____

At the End of Your Day

How did I apply this quote today?

____

____

____

What will I do differently going forward?

____

____

____

"Today most poverty-stricken Americans have a television, telephone, electricity, running water, and indoor plumbing. Most Africans do not. If you transferred the goods and services enjoyed by those who live in California poverty to the average Somalian living on less than a $1.25 a day, that Somalian is suddenly fabulously rich." - Peter H. Diamandis, Abundance: author of The Future is Better Than You Think

Beginning Your Day
What does this quote mean to me personally today?

____

____

____

How will I apply this quote today?

____

____

____

Who else needs to hear this quote today?

____

____

____

At the End of Your Day
How did I apply this quote today?

____

____

____

What will I do differently going forward?

____

____

____

"If you are the kind of person who is waiting for the 'right' thing to happen, you might wait for a long time. It's like waiting for all the traffic lights to be green for five miles before starting the trip." -Robert Kiyosaki, educator on business and personal finance

Beginning Your Day

What does this quote mean to me personally today?

____

____

____

How will I apply this quote today?

____

____

____

Who else needs to hear this quote today?

____

____

____

At the End of Your Day

How did I apply this quote today?

____

____

____

What will I do differently going forward?

____

____

____

"If we are not a little bit uncomfortable every day, we're not growing. All the good stuff is outside our comfort zone." -Jack Canfield, inspirational writer and speaker

Beginning Your Day

What does this quote mean to me personally today?

____

____

____

How will I apply this quote today?

____

____

____

Who else needs to hear this quote today?

____

____

____

At the End of Your Day

How did I apply this quote today?

____

____

____

What will I do differently going forward?

____

____

____

"The Constitution only gives people the right to pursue happiness. You have to catch it yourself." -Benjamin Franklin, publisher, scientist, & co-author of the Declaration of Independence

Beginning Your Day

What does this quote mean to me personally today?

____
____
____

How will I apply this quote today?

____
____
____

Who else needs to hear this quote today?

____
____
____

At the End of Your Day

How did I apply this quote today?

____
____
____

What will I do differently going forward?

____
____
____

"Darkness cannot drive out darkness; only light can do that. Hate cannot drive out hate; only love can do that." -Martin Luther King, Jr., key leader in the civil rights movement of the 1960s

Beginning Your Day

What does this quote mean to me personally today?

____

____

____

How will I apply this quote today?

____

____

____

Who else needs to hear this quote today?

____

____

____

At the End of Your Day

How did I apply this quote today?

____

____

____

What will I do differently going forward?

____

____

____

"Most long-range forecasts of what is technically feasible in future time periods dramatically underestimate the power of future developments because they are based on what I call the intuitive linear view of history rather than the historical exponential view." -Ray Kurzweil, futurist, author of The Singularity is Near

Beginning Your Day
What does this quote mean to me personally today?

How will I apply this quote today?

Who else needs to hear this quote today?

At the End of Your Day
How did I apply this quote today?

What will I do differently going forward?

"By enriching the carbon-dioxide content of the atmosphere from its impoverished pre-industrial levels, human beings have increased the productivity of the entire biosphere - so much so that roughly one out of every seven living things on the planet owes its existence to the marvelous improvement in nature that humans have effected." -Robert Zubrin, aerospace pioneer and proponent of Mars settlement

Beginning Your Day

What does this quote mean to me personally today?

____

____

____

How will I apply this quote today?

____

____

____

Who else needs to hear this quote today?

____

____

____

At the End of Your Day

How did I apply this quote today?

____

____

____

What will I do differently going forward?

____

____

____

"I am always doing that which I cannot do, in order that I may learn how to do it." -Pablo Picasso, artist

Beginning Your Day

What does this quote mean to me personally today?

____

____

____

How will I apply this quote today?

____

____

____

Who else needs to hear this quote today?

____

____

____

At the End of Your Day

How did I apply this quote today?

____

____

____

What will I do differently going forward?

____

____

____

"I confess that in 1901, I said to my brother Orville that man would not fly for 50 years." -Wilbur Wright, co-inventor of the airplane with Orville [in 1903, Orville Wright won a coin toss and preceded his brother as the first documented person to make a powered airplane flight]

Beginning Your Day

What does this quote mean to me personally today?

____

____

____

How will I apply this quote today?

____

____

____

Who else needs to hear this quote today?

____

____

____

At the End of Your Day

How did I apply this quote today?

____

____

____

What will I do differently going forward?

____

____

____

"Hardships often prepare ordinary people for an extraordinary destiny." -C.S. Lewis, author and philosopher

Beginning Your Day

What does this quote mean to me personally today?

____

____

____

How will I apply this quote today?

____

____

____

Who else needs to hear this quote today?

____

____

____

At the End of Your Day

How did I apply this quote today?

____

____

____

What will I do differently going forward?

____

____

____

"The sea, the great unifier, is man's only hope. Now, as never before, the old phrase has a literal meaning: we are all in the same boat." -Jacques Yves Cousteau, oceanic explorer and popularizer

Beginning Your Day

What does this quote mean to me personally today?

____

____

____

How will I apply this quote today?

____

____

____

Who else needs to hear this quote today?

____

____

____

At the End of Your Day

How did I apply this quote today?

____

____

____

What will I do differently going forward?

____

____

____

"You don't have to be great at something to start, but you have to start to be great at something."
-Zig Zigler, author, salesman, and motivational speaker

Beginning Your Day
What does this quote mean to me personally today?

____
____
____

How will I apply this quote today?

____
____
____

Who else needs to hear this quote today?

____
____
____

At the End of Your Day
How did I apply this quote today?

____
____
____

What will I do differently going forward?

____
____
____

"Here's to the crazy ones, the misfits, the rebels, the troublemakers, the round pegs in the square holes, the ones who see things differently. They're not fond of rules. You can quote them, disagree with them, glorify or vilify them, but the only thing you can't do is ignore them because they change things? The ones crazy enough to think that they can change the world are the ones who do." -Steve Jobs, co-founder of Apple Computer, developer of the I-phone

Beginning Your Day

What does this quote mean to me personally today?

____

____

____

How will I apply this quote today?

____

____

____

Who else needs to hear this quote today?

____

____

____

At the End of Your Day

How did I apply this quote today?

____

____

____

What will I do differently going forward?

____

____

____

"You were not put here to live a mediocre life. You were put here to shine." -Michael Stevenson, trainer in hypnotism, neurolinguistics programming language, and business

Beginning Your Day

What does this quote mean to me personally today?

____

____

____

How will I apply this quote today?

____

____

____

Who else needs to hear this quote today?

____

____

____

At the End of Your Day

How did I apply this quote today?

____

____

____

What will I do differently going forward?

____

____

____